Issue 18-1
Winter 2018

Copyright © 2018 *Gyroscope Review*
Constance Brewer & Kathleen Cassen Mickelson
gyroscopereview.com

All rights reserved. No part of this publication may be reproduced or transmitted in any form or by any means, electronic or mechanical, including photocopy, recording, or any information storage retrieval system, without permission from the editors.

For information about permission to reproduce selections from this magazine, contact the editors by email at gyroscopereview@gmail.com.

Submissions: *Gyroscope Review* accepts previously unpublished contemporary poetry submissions through our online submissions system, gyroscopereview.submittable.com/submit. Please read our guidelines before submitting.

For further information, visit our website: gyroscopereview.com.

Editors: Constance Brewer and Kathleen Cassen Mickelson
Logo design: Constance Brewer
Cover art and layout: Constance Brewer
Interior layout and copyediting: Kathleen Cassen Mickelson
Interior artwork: Constance Brewer

FROM THE EDITORS

Welcome to the first issue of *Gyroscope* Review for 2018, our second year of offering print editions, and our looming third anniversary (in April) of being a journal for contemporary poetry.

The poems sent to us for consideration for this issue managed to theme themselves. Submissions are more political than they were when we began this adventure. We are not surprised; poetry is and will always offer a way to reflect on current events, content as well as discontent, and a vehicle for examining memory in the light of now. Editor Constance Brewer, who creates the order in which the poems appear in our pages, had the pleasure of using her drawing skills to create a cover that suited this shift in tone. Constance and co-editor Kathleen Cassen Mickelson brainstormed the cover idea when they got together at Kathleen's home in Minnesota last summer. How could we resist a slightly subversive expression of how we and many others feel about what is happening in our world? Hints trickled out on social media - yes, all those underground references were directly related to groundhogs - for months. So, when submissions lived up to the idea of underground movements of all sorts (resistance, memory, love, anger, hope), we were delighted. And we know that these kinds of poems will keep being written at a fever pitch until poets and those they represent are heard on issues that affect us all: equality, justice, kindness, compassion.

While we do not specifically recruit poets from any defined sector of the population, we are proud that our pages offer a place for poets of many backgrounds. Of the 42 poets represented in this issue, 26 are women. As a woman-owned publication, that statistic is one of our favorites. We also don't just publish poets with MFAs; we offer a voice to poets who came to poetry by other routes, both direct and circuitous. The most important thing about using the poet's voice, in our minds, is the attention paid to word use, to image use, to a path toward some new understanding. And these poets wield their voices with skill. They range from college students to high school teachers to pastors to retired people from all kinds of fields. They are truly the people's voice.

So go make yourself a cup of tea or pour a glass of wine. Settle into your favorite chair. Then crack open our pages and get ready to spend time thinking long and hard about what it is that lodges deep in our minds only to re-emerge as a sign of new growth.

Constance Brewer
Kathleen Cassen Mickelson
January 2018

Gyroscope Review
Issue 18-1: Winter 2018
Table of Contents

Section 1

Hailstorm over Keld by Catherine Edmunds	5
Zen Meditation by Alex Apuzzo	6
Little Runs for Short Loss by Adam Prince	7
Standing at the Kitchen Sink While Being Serenaded by a Choir of Angels Trying to Sing Me Into Existence, Even Though They Know I Think I'm Making This Up by Lyndi Bell O'Laughlin	8
After a Spat by Sarah Merrow	9
Folding by Lenny Lianne	10
A Larcenous Streak Runs in My Family by Jen Sage-Robison	11
The Dental Hygienist Shares the Pain by stephanie roberts	13
Heritage by Samara Golabuk	14
A Valediction Forbidding Despair by T.M. De Vos	15
My bi-polar bear by Paul Strohm	16
Mothersong by Laurinda Lind	17
Memory by Sandra Kohler	18
Memory by Lizzie Bradley	22
Winter Thought by Oonah Joslin	23
Snowfall by Ronald E. Shields	24

Close to the Ground — 25
by Diana Cole

Train Wreck — 26
by Steve Klepetar

Rain Delay: Pace of Play — 27
by Bruce Robinson

What the Lake Knows — 28
by Joanne Esser

Section 2

When the Water — 33
by Kate Hutchinson

The Vault of Seeds — 34
by Sarah Merrow

Early Winter Angel Char — 35
by Tricia Knoll

The Peasant's Tomb — 36
by T.M. De Vos

Chili Burger — 37
by Sylvia Cavanaugh

malleable #1 — 39
by henry 7. reneau, jr.

Commemoration — 40
by Diane G. Martin

Pieces of The Dark — 41
by Jerrice J. Baptiste

Value Meal — 42
by Samara Golabuk

Winter — 43
by Diana Cole

Crime Scene, New York City, 2010 — 44
by Maureen Daniels

A Person of More Means — 45
by Wanda Morrow Clevenger

Edifice — 46
by Peter Arvan Manos

Scattering fragments — 47
by Mike Jurkovic

You — 49
by Irena Pasvinter

The Exhausted Land by Steve Klepetar	50
Ignorance is Bliss by Ed Werstein	51
After by Rush Rankin	52

Section 3

How to Build a Bridge by Samara Golabuk	59
In Blue Velvet, Consumed by Joni Renee	60
Shirley Jackson was My First Analyst by Sylvia Cavanaugh	61
In Winter, In Mayhem by Catherine Edmunds	62
Confronting the Enemy by Carl "Papa" Palmer	63
isolophobia by Wanda Morrow Clevenger	64
How Does a Poem Work? by Samuel Son	65
Healing by T.M. De Vos	67
Weekend Warrior by Andy Macera	68
Prettier Skinnier Smarter by Andy Macera	70
Part for Me by stephanie roberts	71
Today's Bird by Lenny Lianne	73
Flying over Pluto by Bill West	75
Stage by Diane G. Martin	76
this morning the chill is filled with sparrows by Matthew W. Schmeer	77
Observing the Narcissist in its Natural Habitat by Jin Cordaro	78

Good Girl by Samantha Jacobs	79
Begin Again by Laura Madeline Wiseman	80
Intervals by Laurinda Lind	85
Contributors	87
Announcements	93

POEMS

Section 1

HAILSTORM OVER KELD
by Catherine Edmunds

Away too long, I come home and cry out loud
in agony and shame as a hailstorm sweeps down the dale
and the sun—oh God! The sun! Cutting through,
so that the green hurts me, like the glint of a knife; like spite.
I picture her, too much lipstick, too red, a mad harlot, I laugh
at the image; its opposition to the utter green of the land.

This is how a wet floor swells and warps,
this message on his phone that never arrives. I'll get home,
the sheets will be cold, and nothing will warm me.

I've returned too late, stumbling down the steep road,
past the last milestone and into Stalling Busk;
the fells are white and copper in the evening light,
the snow will settle. The ache will spread, the need
to reach the last cottage will break my heart. My limbs
are flimsy, boots have split, ice-water steals my toes.
I will wait till the cottages vanish in the approaching snow.

ZEN MEDITATION
by Alex Apuzzo

I practice Zen Meditation while I crush
garlic with the edge of my knife.
I exercise mindfulness as I slip
papery skin from meaty cloves, and
the blade catches the flesh beneath
my fingertips, and pulls – I
spill my blood into the dish
for the beauty of it.

LITTLE RUNS FOR SHORT LOSS
BY ADAM PRINCE

The guy's *name* is Little, and it's football terminology. You hadn't been paying the right kind of attention, and you can't

go spending your time thinking about whether Mr. Little's name has always held him back. You can't go spending your time thinking how maybe it's been a good thing, tempering his ambitions, since he didn't have the stuff to go pro. He had other stuff. The stuff of the owner of a really nice deli. With good sandwiches. Ones people talked about. The Reuben. You can't,

because your kid is yelling for more chips, and your wife is saying no, the kid's too fat already. And the sun is in your eyes and the field is a hard, hypernatural green. And the Midwest horizon cuts them in two.

STANDING AT THE KITCHEN SINK WHILE BEING SERENADED BY A CHOIR OF ANGELS TRYING TO SING ME INTO EXISTENCE, EVEN THOUGH THEY KNOW I THINK I'M MAKING THIS UP
BY LYNDI BELL O'LAUGHLIN

God's pupils—lagoon water
where I stand, but can't see my feet.
For all I know
a gator is sliding towards me
along the silty bottom,
weaving in and out of willows,
tree trunk tail kicking up iron eyeballs
that linger before a slow sink.

Everywhere, sea-sick swamp angels—
who have nevertheless
launched into their daily aria,
even while trying to hold
their footing in the heavy gumbo
of my inability to feel loved.

I peel an apple.
The angels are giving it
their best shot;
I can taste them in the first juicy bite.
Think what you will.
They can see right into the
cloud shoe of my dead father,
who used to roll the stiff cuff
of his pant leg to use as an ashtray,
because he didn't believe in leaving
traces of himself anywhere.

AFTER A SPAT
BY SARAH MERROW

Never too drunk to knit a sock,
        cinch yarn around needle and *tug*
    on double-wrapped stitches,

those holes at the ankle that
        keep coming around,
    row after row, intractable. They *will*

be tacked shut. Place glass,
        good and empty, on floor
    to catch the ivy's persistent drips --

click-clacks singing "hydrated, hy-dray-ted,"
        while a farmer's wife
    hacks blindly at mice.

Cast yarn at the next pointed stick
        (fiercely as possible
    at two a.m.,) then the next, for

there's always a point. Just knit
        and repeat the pattern,
    oh man, the mad pattern.

FOLDING
BY LENNY LIANNE

Through her window, she senses the nodding
      of low branches,

the world outside refusing to hold still.

At the lean side of the table, she practices
the patterns over and over.

                Corner touching corner,

and then smooth down the cloth napkin
      in one measured gesture

as if each fold evolves into an elaborate spell,
      some sort of sublime reassembly.

Each motion demands an exactness

equal to pulling the extraordinary from one world
      to another.

When her hands spread out,
what's let loose is

      a stranded boat,
      the silent flute of a lily
            or sometimes

      one flattened heart.

She keeps on, completely absorbed
      in this domestic origami.

As the evening passes, she folds into herself

the way a leaf ungreens,
disentangles and settles down.

A LARCENOUS STREAK RUNS IN MY FAMILY
BY JEN SAGE-ROBISON

Nanny ripped candlesticks off the hearth of the Yankee Pedlar Inn,
stuck them on her mantle. She hustled a crystal punchbowl out the front doors
another night, right past the maître d'. She never would say how.
Mom's a master too. Flatware. Small statuary. Flora.
She slipped a platter into her purse at the rooftop café of le Pompidou
while asking directions of a Frenchman. I watched her do it.

Thievery slinks down my maternal line. "I'm liking the look of that butter dish,"
my mother murmurs out the side of her mouth, elbowing my eight-year-old.

We don't just steal from strangers.
Once Nanny stood at the Smith Street sink, elbows in Palmolive
as her living room rug bobbed by the window, rolled over Uncle Kenny's shoulder.
Boompa worked the machine shop then.
With three girls to dress and feed, a good rug was no small thing.
But muted, in crying stitches at Kenny's nerve,
Nanny could only watch as her rug made a get-a-way up the drive.

In the years my mother and I didn't speak, I visited on Thursdays,
when I knew Jeanne, the woman who cleaned, would be in the house alone.
Protected by my mother's horror at letting the cleaning lady know our family had torn,
I slipped in while Jeanne vacuumed and acted like I still had a key.

I stole my mother's sweaters, two sizes too small for me, but smelling of her
perfume and breath. I nabbed the 8X10 of me and Casey off my father's dresser.
Posed on a tan carpeted step at Olin Mills in matching Easter frocks, it was from that early series
in which my sister wore a perpetually stunned look in her infant eyes and a cut lip.
I purloined lawn furniture, wheeled a heavy metal table off the back deck and down
the middle of the drive, wrestled it into the hatch of my Hyundai and drove it back to the city
where it didn't fit on my porch so I positioned it in my cramped yard. I had no chairs
but set a pot of johnny-jump-ups in its middle and watched it through my kitchen window.

Nine years later, when my mother and I reconvened over grandchildren and what I believed
then was forgiveness, we were eager to make reparations.
There were daily telephone calls, books of pasted photographs,
ginger trips to a house on the shore. My mother wrote down the steps to Nanny's apple crisp - the kind with oats, for the ancestral rösti and the sour cream twists baked only in winter,
a lavish reward.

We never spoke of what was stolen or what's still missing.
That's the code among us thieves.

THE DENTAL HYGIENIST SHARES THE PAIN
BY STEPHANIE ROBERTS

Because I know I'm often misread, I go into it prepared
to act more friendly than I am—hopefully, avoiding
the reaming I once earned in a Caribbean Commonwealth,
journeying through customs, after surviving a code red
head-cold and air travel. That customs agent took vocal
offence to my horse-whipped smile. So when the hygienist
starts telling me about her ex-husband's affair, I don't
ask her to stop—as I long to. Nor do I reveal I have
a hard time with strangers touching me. Instead,
I make the interested noise, you know, that *uh-huh* if
you're American and the *mm-hmm* of Canucks. I don't
reveal how I hate to leave my anchoress manor
—stretching what should be an annual visit into the biennial.
I don't say that if she will be quiet I can stare
out the fifth floor window (high by local standards),
and watch hawks and planes feeling the conflation
of flight and spring that blooms red into blues.
If wanting silence makes me an asshole, then I am.
Today I make the noise and she tells me
she had no idea. *We had sex all the same.*
Casting her voice lower she amends: *Actually, it
was even more towards the end,* and I wonder how
these lay together. No idea and the sudden entry
of ardent stallion bucking in the old marital grease?
This is not the place to be a scalpel—to call bullshit
on bullshit; I'm getting my: Plays Nice With Others badge
today come hell or high water. I won't say people
change places without changing. Real change is like
the tide pulling in on a tsunami. I make the good sound.
I leave the good impression. My dentist doesn't chitchat
(god bless); his silent ministry takes me to
the crimson quiet of tulips the river bursting his ice coat
every two years around this time.

Heritage
by Samara Golabuk

Defying the geometry of God,
Lot's wife looked back
and gathered all the salts
of the Dead Sea into her skin,
longing for her daughters
to follow, her eyes cast
backward like a rope,
though that is not how history tells it.

                    How typical
of men to sculpt women as bromide
pillars in the shape of their own lust,
a shape we may coincidentally
take on occasion. So what.

                    Lilith
got a bad rap, too, she sits
on our other shoulder,
fruitless and cunning,
pulling herself into being
out of her own cunt,
yoni ourobouros.

And we sit at the midpoint, our heritage half-mother-wife, half motherless whore
of all life, all loving and all curling smiles
vining around the families we make for ourselves
that lift us on a pillar towards a sky
curved like a comma, holding us
in its bent arm, whispering its
secret longing into our
throbbing, fertile, rising hearts.

A Valediction Forbidding Despair
by T.M. De Vos

I see how it is: seasons
and days that are especially hard
or easier than expected
due to snow or holidays
or someone calling in.
Most food is the same color
and you will never finish
the filing, or mending.
You start to resemble the people
you see in restaurants: skin-faced, chewing.

Your stories all end the same:
spoils going always
to one who cheated, cut in line.
You would have been great,
had the world not been full
of people trading bribes.

And a few times you thought,
maybe after some wine,
that you understood something,
that your spouse should feel a little tragic
over pairing off in the void.

You will never be painted
or asked for your signet;
you have no right to the tectonic plate
beneath your yard or
the gold your money stands for.

There are too many of us
to drown in amber:
they don't even keep the bones.

MY BI-POLAR BEAR
BY PAUL STROHM

She talks as fast as a speeding bullet
her hand gestures could clean the windows of a 60 storied building
and when she forgets her medication she flies to the moon

I pushed her through the neighborhood in a plastic wheelbarrow
we played hide and seek in my Dodge caravan
she slept in the crawlspace between me and the mattress
now she lectures me about things and people she can't possibly know

There's one pill at 6pm another pill before bed and one at 6am
she seldom gets up before noon, what type of life for a 16 year old
but she has such grandiose plans-Europe travel etc etc etc

I seldom sleep as sound as I should and I'm getting old
every new day gets longer, the clock doesn't stop there's never a pause
like walking in a room filled with precious glass with your eyes closed
something is going to get broken, there'll be shards on the floor

She sees all her problems as animated super villains
one day it is Brainiac the next it is Godzilla and Mothra
an endless supply of monsters on the back lot of her emotions

Sometimes we laugh and joke and everything is fine
then in a flash bombs start to go off and there's no place to hide
she threatens the sky with fingers scratching the clouds
I huddle inside myself clutching shared memories she's forgotten

MOTHERSONG
BY LAURINDA LIND

The older I get,
the more we're like,
parts of our luck

kept like cash in
a cup not adding
up, the wrong rows

we planted & now
need to root out by
hand. All our harms

hardened harsh &
blunt like boards we
piled out in the yard.

But we'll dig down
through to granite
& build up again

from there—first
we'll fill our pockets
with greens & balm

& pieces of song in
case we ever learn
how to sing them.

Memory
by Sandra Kohler

i.

The promised snow comes, a pretty snow,
wet, clinging, all the trees coated, each branch,
each twig picked out in white definition.

I brood about why my memories of childhood,
of my teens, twenties, are so dim, incomplete,
vague. I've turned them off.

Could I turn them on? Are they somewhere,
"there," wherever "there" is? What would
trigger them, or pieces of them?

ii.

Sun filtering in from the east touches the pin
oak on the sidewalk, the tops of gingko trees
along the street. Something surfaces: a glint
of sunlight on a river, river on which I'm afloat
in a small rowboat. It's Oakland, New Jersey,
it's summer, the summer after my mother died.
I've been sent to stay with an "old" couple
(old to me) who were friends of my parents.
A boy they know, a few years older than me
- fifteen or so - is taking me for this boat ride
on the river. He's beautiful in my memory,
a young blond god, and kind. Someone must
have recruited him to be kind to this child,
awkward not quite teen-ager, who's just lost
her mother. I'm there, in the boat, I feel the
sunshine, see it moving on the moving river.

iii.

This morning I would like to be writing
the wind and the rain, a flood, storm,
gale, a tropical wash of words coming from
I don't know where, transforming winter's
landscape. Last night my husband and I
talk at dinner over a second glass of wine
about decisions, regrets. He's better at
regretting than I am, more prone to it.
Happily he doesn't regret marrying me.
Do I not allow myself regrets because if
I did I'd find so much to rue it would be
overwhelming? Is not regretting the reason
my memory of parts of my past is so dim?

iv.

I can feel the air in the room I'm in, a room in
someone's Queens apartment, fifty years ago,
a group of people there: Frank Alwaise, John,
Harry, Richard. I don't know if there's anyone
else. Last week John and Harry emailed to say
that Frank had died; I hadn't thought of him
in decades. The four were friends in high school,
John and Harry were my friends too, Richard
my boyfriend, later my husband. He's been dead
for thirty-seven years. Frank and John and Harry
and Richard are talking about putting on a play,
The Crucible. The room's full of smoke – is
the smoker Frank? – of dark colors, – my clothes,
the couch covers, curtains? I'm feeling something
dark and uncomfortable but I don't know what.
Jealousy? Insecurity? Possessiveness? A desire
to be a success at what we're doing, whatever
that is? It's lost in the backward reach of time.

v.

Reading the Odyssey, I think of my life these
days as an odyssey of loss, lessening, a shrinking
world and consciousness. Not true but feared.
I am becoming the old woman I only imagine,
don't feel myself being. She's real. She wears
a purple coat too big for her, like her skin,
she looks frail and shrunken, her face is lined
and pouched and sagging like her skin, breasts;
her hair is gray and thin, she's smaller than
she was for years, diminished, slight. She is
the monster I meet, the threat I can't escape.

vii.

Now that our two grandchildren are both
out of diapers, I have reclaimed the bureau
in our bedroom where we changed them,
bureau we bought as a changing table for
our son, their father, when he was an infant.
I'm covering it with thisses and thats – an
oil lamp, a glass lantern, the white bud vase
my daughter-in-law gave me years ago with
two paper flowers our granddaughter made
for us in it, two small photographs: my son
at eleven or so, its frame the leather one he
made in Boy Scouts, the other with his wife
on their wedding day, in a small silver frame.

viii.

In a carved wooden box that was a drawer
of an old sewing machine, I've stashed a tin
of rosebud salve, its scent dense, familiar,
lovely. Where have I smelled it before?
Could my mother have possibly used it?
Could I invent a mother who did, a woman
tender, softer than the mother I remember,
who was hardened and dried by fear, by
suffering, by the bitter knowledge inflicted
on her which she inflicted on me?

ix.

I would like the past to be a puzzle,
a crossword that slowly becomes clearer
as you work it, about which you have
sudden illuminations, moments of
recognition, knowledge you didn't
know you had surfacing, becoming
clear, lucid, making sense. This is
what I'd like the past to be. It's not.

MEMORY
BY LIZZIE BRADLEY

My earliest is a Sea World that no longer exists. Two years old, I sit on my mother's lap in a concrete stadium. Dolphins arc over us, soaring in high parabolas. My eyes stay on them. They fade into the yellow stadium backdrop that fades into clouds that fade into sunlight — A shift. Orcas now. They splash, tumble like acrobats. Black rubber bodies that move through clear membranes: water, air, glass dividers. Osmosis. They swim downward without gravity. The salt-stained tank is the deepest thing in the world. My mother lifts me up to see. I watch their bodies warp, shrink, disappear down, down into the cold water. Gone forever. Belugas breach the surface.

WINTER THOUGHT
BY OONAH JOSLIN

There's some little thought
in the cold that fills the crevasses of winter.
Something we are taught
by summer's bright mentor.

In the deep of winter
some seed is left behind
by summer's mentor,
residual and kind.

This gift that's left behind
of warmth and greenery
reminds us to be kind
sharp as holly, red in berry.

Warmth we give, and greenery
this time of year, and so we ought;
spices, red wine, all things bright and merry
and of course, some little thought.

SNOWFALL
BY RONALD E. SHIELDS

It is the covering of things.

Heavy curtains pulled shut,
girls in wool coats.
A bear's eyelids close.

There is the falling –
icy, unbearable lightness,

the imprints of boots,
angel's wings,

the weight of mountains in trees,
of hummingbirds on my tongue.

The bones in my hands
sink beneath the weight of feathers.

CLOSE TO THE GROUND
BY DIANA COLE

> *A wild field of mushrooms is growing.*
> *At the local cemetery there is weeping.*
> — Jared Lee Loughner*

Fruiting bodies rise overnight
    on leaf rot,
       damp ground.
Mushrooms, some mind-altering,
like the Fly Agaric used by the Vikings
to invigorate the battle.
      If one dies
        another takes its place.

Take the Amanita Virosa
    large, flaring, persistent
    known as the Death Angel,
popping up everywhere,
markets, the stadium
at some music festival.
    It pulls a switch,
      takes aim from a window.

The new numbers rise overnight too,
    58 in Las Vegas
    49 in Orlando.
The daily tally deadened
by the familiar voice over the radio,
moving on briskly to report
    the traffic on the Southeast Expressway,
    rain for the weekend.

*lines from a poem by Jared Lee Loughner, the Tucson shooter.

TRAIN WRECK
BY STEVE KLEPETAR

Who am I to sit by the window and laugh
as a train out of some gray city
lurches off tracks on the river bridge?

I'm no monster, but you have to admit
it's been a slow fall
long time coming, always a comedy

as long as bodies dive from windows
to splash wet and discomfited in traveling
clothes, bobbing like seals among rocks

as the river loops around a point and disappears.
But still, winter rushes toward us,
hidden in these warm days, its icy incisors

sharp as ever in the camouflaged wind.
Say we've brought warm clothing
down from the attic, and our wood pile

stretches along the house.
Say our fences remain strong, the gate
bolted and chained.

Say canned goods bulge in the cupboards
and we manage to sleep with an eye
toward the changing moon.

It's good to be prepared for movement
at the tree line, for the rattle of drums,
for flags and fires ripping through the heart of night.

RAIN DELAY: PACE OF PLAY
BY BRUCE ROBINSON

Put a clock on

      it, why not, like everything else-

– time redefined –

      as if acceleration could
forestall the inevitable
      (yes, still raining) running down of

the universe.

WHAT THE LAKE KNOWS
BY JOANNE ESSER

"In nature, the answers are always changing."
-Tom Hennen

Walking with my longtime friend in the last
days of winter, we lament the recent
turns of events, how hatred has bubbled up
as if from underground, spilling onto
the earth, winding its way in spreading
torrents across our feet, the terror
of its rising, rising above our ankles.

The unnatural swell of constant bad news
batters like stirred-up stormtide the borders of
our minds and hearts, our skin, and though
we try to stay alert, unguarded, we both admit
we're hardening, starting to wall-off the waves
of voices: the hurt, the ignored, the betrayed,
to try to protect ourselves from the surge.

Quiet now, we walk the path around the lake
that is still holding onto a sheen of ice;
who knows what stirs beneath its surface.
All at once the ice on the lake
thunders, rumbling surprising booms,
easy to mistake for distant traffic noise
unless someone lets you in on the secret.

My friend stops me. We listen together.
She is a woman of the north woods
and knows the language of the lake
as it shudders under its frozen layer,
beginning to shrug off its winter weight.
I can hardly believe my beloved water
speaks with such a guttural voice.

I have only heard its whispers, its summer
gentle song, the pulse of small waves.
This groan is so much deeper, with
startling power I've never realized.
Change is coming, it rumbles
with the wisdom of one who has witnessed
all of this many times before,

as it stirs with the patient knowledge
of inevitable thaw.

Section 2

WHEN THE WATER
BY KATE HUTCHINSON

After the hurricane we saw photos of people
lining highways with their boats, waiting.
They motored slowly into the flooded streets
like t-shirted gondoliers calling out to the silent
rooftops, an armada of eyes and ears.

There, an old couple in life vests held hands.
There, a dog straddled a tree branch, a mother
clutched her child atop a sofa, half-submerged.
Brown water swirled, then stilled, stubbornly
believing it belonged in dens and nurseries.

~ ~ ~

In Greenland some narwhal hunters
tell reporters that ice sheets were only
three inches thick this year, too fragile
for dog sleds. They fish now in kayaks
or hunt for walrus in berg-riddled fjords.

Amid echoes of calving from gray glaciers,
families in Qaanaaq share the meager catch
with dogs who stretch and whine with ennui.
Now, they say, they must rely on the kindness
of occasional outsiders. Or simply pray.

~ ~ ~

The people at this party get younger every year.
With wired ears and electronic palms
they signal each other in new languages,
clustering at the bar glowing green with neon,
their faces frozen in silent-movie laughter.

When it's clear that I have become invisible,
I escape the patio to find the pier, under lattices
of golden locust leaves, then step into a canoe.
I row to the center of the lake where all is still—
in my head a forgotten song. My son's face.

THE VAULT OF SEEDS
BY SARAH MERROW

The underground Svalbard Global Seed Vault, built in 2008 about 620 miles from the North Pole, is a frozen-storage facility for the world's most important crop seeds. ...a backup for gene banks around the world, protecting genetic material from natural disasters, war and other problems. Thus, the moniker "doomsday vault." In May 2017, the entrance to the vault was breached by melted ice-water, the result of a warm winter and thawing permafrost.

The dream consists of baby goats
hopping all over time. Hey, kids!
I shout, ecstatic, carefree with
the promise of new beginnings

hopping all over time. Hey, kids!
In white silence we bounce around
the hillside, jostling between
thought and sleep in our taut glee.

In white silence we bounce around
dreaming, and I wonder what
the trees would say, black branches
tossing in the night. No longer

dreaming, I wonder what
their muteness means, what other joy
is this quiet, maybe seeds on ice in
an arctic vault, waiting out the rain.

EARLY WINTER ANGEL CHAR
BY TRICIA KNOLL

Trust reluctance
  of the falling fog season
  to give way to slow sun dying,
  to iced twigs.

Trust the sighing
  of ragged grasses,
  looming nights de-lighted,
  creek rising to torrent.

Trust how fleeting
  has-been leaves clog
  cement drains
  and flood the crow street ballet.

Trust what changes
  the twist of the worm
  pulls a last leaf to the lair,
  leaves frass behind the praying mantis.

Trust what does not change
  snow blindness on a revelation morning
  sheen of a raven wing shiver
  last gasps of chrysanthemums and kale.

Trust what you cannot foresee
  high-jump winter fires
  that sullen winds
  do not snuff.

The Peasant's Tomb
by T.M. De Vos

The body is still fresh, separate:
hair unfused, flowers not yet tar.

It tests its cavities;
the gone parts still taste of blood.

In legends, the battered poppet,
having known cruelty
is awarded tissue, a metabolism—
it stumps in its master's place
to war, to the fields,
eyes bright with the glaze of brainstem.

It's the kind of story the poor tell
who believe in some world
where they are not broken,
where they need no food but fumes,
and the soul is bedded like an ox,
ready to pull when it wakes.

CHILI BURGER
BY SYLVIA CAVANAUGH

Full metal throat
of tin can chili
Sunday evening surprise visit
my new neighbor

this food stuff of industry
of industrial decline
clanged against my fillings

his mother's own recipe
one can with meat
one can without
on a toasted bun
topped with American melted

his unfocussed eyes
offered this chili burger
as a gift
or repayment
for the use of my can opener

he opened an age-old pride
his mother's overburden craft

he opened an 8-track cassette tape
opened a Mountain Dew
shelved in the yellowed Frigidaire
my spinster great aunt
kept on hand

she loved the name *Mountain Dew*
spoken in the tongue
of her own Blue Ridge poetry

she cooked on a coal stove
one temperature
seasoned our food with sulfur fume

the way we went skinny dipping
in the skree-cradled alkaline pool
when the strip mine was done

MALLEABLE #1
BY HENRY 7. RENEAU, JR.

the commercial world advertises reality as a selective dream, as oligarchs
pick the entertainments, the celebrities, the presidents & the wars;

& history—where the perfect crime frames the wrong-doer, written in the
language of progress & the machinery of shadow,

moves into the longer light, red & white & blue(s), into the plenty of pain
—a discriminating star spangled banner next to "we shall overcome"

& nobody laughing anymore, 'cause God too preoccupied
& he don't take sides.

the "why?" & "what if?" of dissent, an ostracized human urgency—to
point out things we already know—demeaned in sarcastic jokes

traded by dive bar drunks & conservative pundits; the tempered steel
of common sense & courage

neglected to rust—recycled into sorrow songs like *pin-cushion souls
with glowing perforations*.

& eventually, the holes in our mouths close over like scars
& we never say another word.

Note: fragment in seventh stanza from "Stroke: A Right Hemisphere Love Story" by Julianna Baggott.

COMMEMORATION
BY DIANE G. MARTIN

Build no more hero statues,
no more monuments
to power, to hubris from
materials indestructible.
They can, of course,
be toppled.

And then, what to top
the barren plinth
with? Yet another
warrior or his vanquished
foe? Or endless victims?

Stop commemorating
brutal carnage with
names like "Martyr's Square,"
"Freedom Street," "Museum
of the Revolution."

If you must play architect,
erect instead a school
for fools to learn by heart
the fine arts of starving,
grieving, mourning, leaving.

PIECES OF THE DARK
BY JERRICE J. BAPTISTE

Hungry wolf, I bite into *CLIF* Bar
banana nut bread not part of mother's
language. She asks, *"Are you eating?"*
in our phone conversations,
can't tell her my new language has
cacao listed as ingredient too. Rolls
bitterly under tongue.

I've given up
on the possibility of having
children. *"Are you too skinny?"*
A minister's son wants to
marry me. In a frenzy,
grow my hair, wear ankle
length skirt, carry a bible,
give up swearing. *"No."*

I've learned a new language of man
who clings to edge of cliff, runs on moon
a marathon. Fills my round belly
not with babies but inspiration.

I can write pages
about the preacher's son only
after chewing pieces of the dark.

VALUE MEAL
by Samara Golabuk

Time is a fist,
squeezing me of plum blood
pound by pound, pressed and ground
like tomatoes into sauce, and also
I am the dough—
folded. kneaded, knotted,
flattened, torqued and leavening,
rising against my foil mask.

Roll and flip, toss the disc,
ladle-spread that red
in quick, thick arcs.
I am woman, divide me:
    slice of mother
    slice of worker
    slice of cleaner, listener, fucker, dreamer
section me, and try a piece:
I will form myself from the remains,
crumbs and box and bones.

WINTER
by Diana Cole

Clean-edged houses keep distance.
Fences square off vast white fields
where grass waits to prove green.
Birches, stripped, are candid
against a cobalt sky.
Even the air has teeth.

Just over the rise the sea never freezes,
ever moving in and out over land.
The marsh fills, drains, leaving
crabs and snails to scramble.
An egret probes the icy sedge,
devours what it can before water quickens.

As with words, never a surfeit,
never certainty, only self-rationing urgency.

CRIME SCENE, NEW YORK CITY, 2010
In memory of Karen Schmeer
BY MAUREEN DANIELS

Sirens animate the night,
red, ominous, revolving
on the streams of yellow
tape snapping in the wind.

News vans and police cars
against the curb, the trench-
coated detective cursing
in the emptied street.

A winter coat is lumped
between the lanes of Broadway,
surrounded by a pocketbook
and its contents strewn block-wide,

the smear of a crushed rose
lipstick, the scent of a pocket-
sized perfume, gardenias,
chunks of cars, the broken

heel of a black boot,
and in the median on Broadway,
caught on the branch of a bush, a torn
red blouse, arms splayed, fluttering.

A Person of More Means
by Wanda Morrow Clevenger

come by an
inheritance
higher math
a long-time
torment
I had to
make nice
with stocks
CD's
money market
accounts, dividends
Roth IRA's
interest percentages
total fixed incomes
roll overs
growth, yields
caps
I had to indulge
a personal
9-page portfolio
analysis
I had to think
like a person of
more means
I had to think
outside the
ceramic pig
now that I was
uncomfortably
more comfortable

EDIFICE
BY PETER ARVAN MANOS

From humble excellence
or unpretentious excellence
comes adolescent excellence
some uncontested excellence
plus compartmental excellence
inter-continental excellence
transcendental excellence
condescended excellence
unrepentant excellence
pretentious excellence
obsessive excellence
restless excellence
wearable excellence
reckless excellence
or death or parkour
or obsolesced paragons
of humble excellence
that arrogant parables
couldn't surpass
after good enough
wasn't good enough
and better
wasn't better.

SCATTERING FRAGMENTS
BY MIKE JURKOVIC

What if every father
carries a covert illness
the sons don't see
but inherit?
A hard accounting
no love can allay.

What if no one
gets away easy
and rumination
the new routine;
the daily task?
Leaving none the less
behind.

What if this
is the way it is
for a reason? A wrath?
A dictum sworn before?
A carrion tic
that carries the night.

What if the cows
don't come home
and this is what's left
to forage? To cull from those manic
moments of mercy
some legacy to cosign.

What if the good guys
don't always win
and the mask
falls to the pavement?
Scattering fragments
like tablets of stone.

What if this isn't
nothing but flesh
and bone? Built on a sinking berm
like everything structured
by human hands?
Jerry-rigged
against the code
to which none of us
aspire.

You
by Irena Pasvinter

They say you are all-forgiving,
And merciful, and all that.
They don't mind you torture the living
As long as you save the dead.

They bug you with endless prayers,
Implore you to curse their foes.
They believe if they do as you sayeth,
You'd bless their swords and wombs.

They create and destroy in your name,
Raising money and spilling blood.
And although you might not look the same,
You are always in their heart.

Nowadays you're often alone
Or as three for the same price,
Though it's certainly not unknown
When a crowd of you survives.

Never mind the shape and number.
If you were in critical mood,
You would think it an awful blunder,
This creation of human brood.

They don't get it that you don't care.
You ignore them, but they persist.
Even atheists, when in despair,
Send you prayers as if you exist.

THE EXHAUSTED LAND
BY STEVE KLEPETAR

What stirs in its sleep this cold morning?
What rises in the fog?
All my life I have been in love with words,
those shadows of lip and teeth and tongue.
Now they swirl in a hurricane of noise.
Everything seems broken,

walls trembling in strange wind.
Through a cracked window, fractured sun
sheds its weary light above the trees.
Another storm churns toward the exhausted land.
Somewhere else fires burn. Nothing is far away.
Smoke hangs near enough to taste, pungent as ruined wine.

IGNORANCE IS BLISS
BY ED WERSTEIN

It's better we don't realize our coming doom.
Play a game, watch TV, or drink a glass of wine
as death bides time, lurks hidden in the room.

Thoughts of death will always lead to gloom.
We clear our minds, go out, enjoy the sunshine.
It's better not to think about our approaching doom.

Steadily we march on toward the tomb,
though exercise and eating well keeps us feeling fine.
Still death bides time, lurks hidden in the room.

World War 3, an accident, at best, our old age looms.
Not every lump one finds is diagnosed benign.
Death's biding time, lurks hidden in the room.

We're prefect metaphors for wilting blooms,
stale bread, broken barns, rusted old road signs.
If we only could ignore the coming doom.

There's no doubt we're sliding down a steep incline.
But it makes no sense at all to fuss and fume.
There's no benefit in dwelling on the coming doom.
Death's quite content biding time, lurking hidden in the room.

AFTER
by Rush Rankin

> *Let's talk of graves, of worms, of epitaphs,*
> *Make dust our paper, and with rainy eyes*
> *Write sorrow on the bosom of the earth.*
> *William Shakespeare*

i

On our dusty farm, I killed rabbits, chickens,
and squirrels, whose supplemental role in cartoons
    I never noticed, though at school my drawing
    of the rabbit I ate won a prize. The past, more
expansive than perception, that light pointed
        at the sun, preempts my ability to recall it,
        except in glimpses, a water spider skating
            its vanishing moves across the pond.

In the reflective openness of poetry a specific
        signifies a judgment no idea replaces,
that necessary conclusion beyond proof,
except in glimpses, a water spider skating
        its vanishing moves across the pond.

ii

In the rarefied ontology of a self-defining
tautology, which rhymes, as well it should,
the unique speaks itself: if "$A=A$" it's not
        "B," which is a passing grade, but not
        the best way to describe what's true
            when a vague person whispers.
The mirroring mind a transparent window
reflecting the person looking and his view
induced Aristotle to study crustaceans,
        but not *the children, slaves, and women*
who wore veils: that paper under words.
        At night, without his robe, asleep,
he exposed the limits of Greek thought
in a fraternity house, which saves, for
the future, all the old tests and answers.

iii

       Each theory shifts from the mind of the critic
          framing the work to the work itself enacting
the happening of a life that engulfs the critic
after lunch: his émigré affectations too wistful,
his white tennis shorts too proper. The arcane
      future zooming through its focus, like a guy
falling from a roof, one word at a time, excludes
          all others, as when you order wine.

iv

    The shoe an Iraqi throws through the air
of one culture just misses a guy, a goofy smile
      on his face, standing in another.
Opposed to bi-lingual education in public
schools, a Texas governor said: "After all,
English was good enough for Jesus." Words
vanish like smoke signals in the tribal air.
That a suffering poet puts books in a furnace
to engage readers who pick words from ashes
exposes a nervous version of a tragic history.

v

The bleached corpse in the street, like any cliché
on the nightly news, is still unexpected. Even
a transcendental Emerson, the smiling master
     of gravitas, wrote Thoreau at his pond,
which was quiet, like a park, each path a guide,
to condemn the tuxedo norm of English snobs.

*In the semiotics of semiosis, the fungible
otherness of otherness, the suspended
nominalism of power, of imperialism,
    Robinson Crusoe reads the print
        of a foot, not the sand.*

vi

Through my office window I see the audience
in the cloistered park, in plastic chairs and on
      the grass, watching local actors prepare
Hamlet, as nearby residents, carrying blankets
and baskets, sneak out of the surrounding
      darkness to settle in the extended glow
from the stage. The dazed, dutiful Ophelia,
betraying her lover, suffers in pornographic
songs the phallic imperialism of the time.
Hamlet's so-called friend, Horatio, responds
to each deadly crisis after the fact, like a poet,
content, relaxed, distracted by the Erasmus
      cult of the abstract scholar, as though
           drugged in a house on fire.

vii

That a cell phone sends and accepts messages
      on a plane mimes the magical power

      of ancient gods. A drone, directed
by a woman in Florida, each finger a laser
      designation, separates one ancient hope
from another. A white pickup truck streaking
      across the desert disappears. Averroes,
      the Islamic scholar, displacing the mythic
      dark, rescued the classical Greek
      that Christian scribes neglected.
      Making a fortune for the Vatican
        on donkeys all over Europe,
      monks sold the infinite pieces
        of the last robe of Jesus.

viii

In a testament, a test, the te<u>st</u>es,
or the t<u>setse</u> fly, the fading buzzing
of a sleeping sickness, the Columbian
    proverb explains: "He who dies
        must die in the dark
           even if he sells candles."

ix

    Typing these lines, after sitting for hours
at my narrow, grey wooden desk, the Campaign
      model, a replica of the British army desk
      used in India, an intertext irony, perhaps,
I'm hurled from my swivel chair to the Persian
      rug, an intertext irony, perhaps, both thighs
knotted in pain, in tightening cramps, caused
      by my failure to drink enough water, I bet.

Frantically, I stretch out, frantically I rub my leg.

x

Good manners reflect a history of respect for kind
expressions of regret, just as country blues lament
the sadness of willful neglect, just as a devoted fan
later laps up spilled champagne, like a cat. Poetry.
In their probing relationship and mutual caring,
in the subtle imperfections of even decent people,
in the limits of even the best dogma, in the dark,
in a fog, in a storm, and in their brief happiness,
Huck and Jim, on the other hand, naked on a raft,
expose a soulful longing. The smoke from a cabin
on shore rises and fades like the breath no one sees.

Section 3

How to Build a Bridge
by Samara Golabuk

Unbind from boxes,
wind a water moccasin
around your spine,
grout your way
through relationships.

Mortar and pestle
your viscera into
a paste you can build
with, cultivate
concrete, flirt with
crevasses, see both sides.

Things will move away
from you, always. Court
that distance, learn
to love it, leave
scratches on its back.
Peer over cliff edges,
lean a little too far.

Make your fingertips beetles,
that desperate grip will be true.   Reach.
Suspend tendons from invisible
arcs, and root shoulder beams
against gravity, which seeks no
consent for what it does.

The rest
is not up
to you.

In Blue Velvet, Consumed
by Joni Renee

On some level, everyone hopes they'll live their whole life without finding a dead body. On some level, we'd like to be on motorcycles in June, riding to the wedding of our favorite childhood friend. Am I not the will of the executor? Ask instead why I've been out to the storage unit to put my hands on what we own.

I'm sure I see you on ships: a little book in the hand, a box with a locket, tiny vials inside, sweet oils to dress my curls. To be sure of a thing, you have to believe in the entirety of It (the moment you stop trusting math, all numbers lose their brilliance). Perhaps you've seen the Gorge or the American Dream burning. Our valley fields are covered with antiques, scattered copper pans and window adornments where cows should walk but no longer do. If I swipe over you, will I stop believing in It?

Imagine me, in a skirt like a cover letter, with thyme. Imagine two kissing girls, one Pain, one Potential, in a china cup at a bull auction. Imagine the fibers of strong ropes, rough against thighs. Once our immediate needs are met, your animal can sleep here in my moonlight.

Those dots are the campfires of the gentle people. Welcome to my home! The less complicated girlfriend. In West Linn, a flailing. Repetitive motor movements in an attractive mom community swimming pool. Lay down your seamed and seamless things: prism of ryegrass seeds on the rim of the before-bed lamp, pyramid of dim schooners in the margin.

We could talk about the many terrible things that led us here, but where is here? Name a better barn for fickle hands. Every two weeks on payday I'm ravenous for my handsome surgeon, his nimble fingers on the scalpel, his knowing tongue, his long, wide charts. Every digital bit of the May wages is for him, the learned man who cut me up while the rain fell on theatergoers in Ashland. *"Spring is the only revolutionary whose revolution has succeeded."*

SHIRLEY JACKSON WAS MY FIRST ANALYST
BY SYLVIA CAVANAUGH

Even before I read *The Lottery*
in high school
my number was up
I had come to believe the only way
to pretend to be sane
would be to marry Daedalus after all
I understood the odds
stacked against women who began
as awkward introverted girls
Shirley laid out Eleanor Vance
as exhibit number one
in *The Haunting of Hill House*
when I was eight
and my mother took me too young
to see the film at the college campus
I learned that even mothers
smother in their bitterness
that to be alone is the real cold
dark of hell
that the underworld is not alight
with flame and crowded
in a shared camaraderie of misery
Shirley pressed upon me the danger
of my own mind looking back at itself
from the curved glass of a mirror
careening through off-kilter rooms
crafted by men
that some spaces I dare not enter
libraries and domestic scenes
most lethal
that the voice in my head
lost in a labyrinth
will be loud as a jackhammer
that my scream will be silent

In Winter, In Mayhem
by Catherine Edmunds

Slush-snowy, the ice maze of archipelagos
abating in the slipstream of the fall—I feel
the shift, the harbour moves underground
where drowned catfish hog the waters,
read papers and surf skies, fin deep, feathered and slim.

These are the snow dreams, these
the angels of deafness, and all the time
the lurch, the indescribable grinding.

"Will it snow, do you think?"

But your head's in the paper,
your snuffling moustache
like a cat's arse, your lips—
I once, once, but never again.

Hold this earth, it cannot remain toughened,
like asbestos, it cannot slide without all the laws
absconding, it cannot exist undefined
in the dripdrip-drip of my belly, warm, soft.

You beg in my head and I rant about intangibility,
you scold—we are Nag and Nagaina, we stand
back to back, walk fifty paces, tear out
our entrails, offer them back
and warp them in time, in calamity;
no sunrise, no stooks, no city promenades
of skylining grotesques, and the ice, oh sweet, sweet…

"Yes," you say, "I believe it will."

CONFRONTING THE ENEMY
BY CARL "PAPA" PALMER

What reason do you have to steal into my marriage,
confiscate my husband with your morbid romance,
of all men why did you choose my man, Bitch?

Why bring yourself into our house, disrupt our life,
arrive unexpected, unasked, unwanted, unwarranted,
can't you realize what you're doing to us, Whore?

Why wrangle his thoughts, mangle his memories,
infiltrate his mind, defeat dreams, doom his future,
obscure consciousness, confuse reality, Tramp?

Answer me. Why not come out, confront me, face me,
who are you, what title are you using today, Harlot,
or is it still Alzheimers, Senility or Dementia ?

ISOLOPHOBIA
by Wanda Morrow Clevenger

is fear
of being alone

the telltales
there all along

chalked up to
blindside
nature nurture
twist turn
mortal mangle

not considered
until late
in the game

after the fact
after the end
left alone
to hypothesis

How Does a Poem Work?
by Samuel Son

i'm not sure

but it's what you look for when your father dies
and you were expecting it for awhile,
because he had a full life, the pastor says,
like a pear, ripe with sun,
snaps from the branch
and falls to earth,
and no estranged child,
everyone came
and kissed his face
the week before
he passed away,
ain't that a blessing, amen,
the church people say,
and yet

that emptiness in your
60 year old chest,
is so vast even
the night can't fit in it,
and you don't know how to say it,
so your hands go fumbling through
you old poetry anthology
from college, the one book
you didn't throw away
through all the filtering of your life's
moves, that poem you don't remember
fully but always lingered, all your life,
in the background,
like the dark energy
that keeps everything visible
together, the scientists say

though they're not 100% sure
if that is how the universe works
as i'm not sure, as i admitted
how a poem works

i know how death works

it takes

HEALING
BY T.M. DE VOS

Everything was lifted out:
chairs, a chest of spoons,
the piano, all mice and mouldering hammers.
Suits so full of moths
they flew down on their own
and old ledgers, inked red with shortfalls.
Walls full of razors:
decades of cut men rusting
and scarabs, shy of the shearing edges,
living off the skin.

The wound is an organizing principle:
it draws you in to hunch, and bear it.

Peace is a cold serum
rising through pipes—
a beam of dust,
abiotic, waiting for clearance.

WEEKEND WARRIOR
BY ANDY MACERA

I can hear you whisper
behind the paper thin walls of youth
painted obnoxious shades
of careless and cocky

even though this morning
you panicked over a pimple
staring at it through the binoculars of the mirror
as if trying to identify a rare bird
resting in the field of your face

the first clue that time is coming
the same message I'm preaching
from the broken pulpit of my body

draft me

I'm no fantasy
I'm defense
rebounds
riding the rush of dirty work down low
drawing a charge
diving on the grenade of a loose ball
taking one for the team

never mind the scars
the joints exaggerated by braces
they are wrecked with wisdom

you pretty boys can keep your highlight reel dunks
fancy spin moves and no look passes
lining the endless parade route of your future cheering
the lights green
the shot clock fresh

thinking about a girl you just rolled off of
feeling her ghost legs still wrapped around your back

no one's waiting for me
I've made my choices
it's your turn

in this world you're either a winner or a loser
and you candy asses don't yet know the real difference

look at Jesus
he picked all the wrong guys
I'd never let you hang like that

PRETTIER SKINNIER SMARTER
BY ANDY MACERA

I'd walk past them in the library and
image it's what they were thinking, flipping
through *Seventeen*, their feet up on the edge
of the chair as if digging in to stop the steep
slide into the lowest circle of self-esteem
where the ordinary and average are bathed
in shades of eggshell and ash, far beyond
the afterglow of an airbrush. My friends and
I were gifted, using the stem cells of beer and
bongs to grow what we were missing, gathering
like Kentucky Derby winners on a stud
farm, our faces large screen televisions
howling at the low scores assigned to the
names of these girls whipping around the
uneven bars of our boredom, how they will
cut off toes and heels to fit into glass slippers
or awaken with the gnawed off limbs of
strangers trapped beneath their bodies. In
the lifeboat game, they were always thrown
first into the water. Now, I think of the father
in Kosztolányi's *Skylark* coming home drunk,
finally pulling the harpoon of *we don't love her*
out of his chest, the mother clinging to the
sinking cruise ship of a crucifix.

PART FOR ME
BY STEPHANIE ROBERTS

gulf of mexico.
my knee is strongly against
the tide
of your refusal;
solar flares pizazz
overcast skies
with a nudge
of insistent shine.
i hate to tell you
what comes next;
i hate to tell you
the hard look of helpless
splintering
across your horizon.
which i ignore
like your utterance of: callous.
don't you know?
your every look
is already engraved in me,
scripted along
the black of my right shoulder
you can read it in the dark
by light fingers
or the purple clouds of memory.
anyway, awareness
feeds some childhood terror.
childish
forgive me;
it can't be helped;
black skin burns blue
under the full moon;
salt and caramel
compliment as do
chocolate and chillies.
do you think this is easy for me?
baby, it's a heartbreaker
coaxing spring from frozen soil;
i promise
i'm singing into your

purple wound
as tenderly as i can (which
still seems to pink you).
part for me.
i stay
idling.
give in.
it's holding the ocean
back that aches;
it is the way
you don't want me
to say
what i'm going to say.

TODAY'S BIRD
BY LENNY LIANNE

I hear the bird's harsh thump
as it crashes into the patio window
and see it stand, shake itself a bit,
then walk back into its own world,
its held breath let out again,
as if this hadn't happened today.

It leaves behind a faint imprint,
both wings fanned out, on the glass
like a ghost bird that might have
flown inside, bolted high over
the dinner table, into the kitchen
and out some phantom window.

It reminds me of Bede's sparrow
that glided through time and
came into sight when it flew
through an open window and over
the warm and cheery mead hall,
only to vanish into the winter night.

In the mead hall, with its raucous
guffaws and heroic songs,
with its stomach-warming stew
and plentiful pitchers of wine,
some sang, full-lunged, laments
for all they'd lost or let go,

then shrugged and laughed
as though their own dumb luck
might save them from the icy night.
Too absorbed in their own bloated
moment, not many noticed
the sparrow or heard the whoosh

of its wings as it flew away,
as though it hadn't been ready
to be seen. Elsewhere today's bird
endured the difference between
what's seen and the experience
of what it sees, which could bring
even ghosts to there knees,

the way the window itself,
indifferent to either bird,
stays a place of before, and after.

FLYING OVER PLUTO
BY BILL WEST

I was flying over Pluto
coal black night side
'til light tinged tortoise shell
fragments littered the edge,
a frozen nitrogen sea and
craters like giant paw prints
cartoon faces, eyeless howlers,
blunted range of giant finger nails,
clawed nicotine snow fields
and the remains
of rain-pocked snowmen
sliding into the dark.

STAGE
BY DIANE G. MARTIN

Vagabond player, native city's son,
you rove Moscow's wet, labyrinthine
boulevards, courtyards, muddy alleyways
all day, hungry for bread and tea
and a break, a stake in a new story,
new role, while I dream up dinner,
wondering if you'll show after plunging

below, denizen of the metro.
Later, when you're steeped in stupor,

if I scraped off a geological
sample from your damp, battered boots,
shed on the hall rug like an extra skin,
could I trust the encrusted layers—like
a scientific oracle—
to reveal to me the haunts where you've been
and why you can't stop wandering?

THIS MORNING THE CHILL IS FILLED WITH SPARROWS
by Matthew W. Schmeer

small light this morning
as the chill comes down
in drafts, the moon a plate

in fading darkness
too many stars
dimpling the clouds

and I creep out the door
into grass stained wet,
feel the stones shift

black branches smack
my face and arms
as I trace the path

to the car, the spotlight
flashing my shadow
across the concrete's fissures

a host of sparrows take
leave, their crumbs
fodder for the coming crow

OBSERVING THE NARCISSIST IN ITS NATURAL HABITAT
BY JIN CORDARO

It lives alone but depends on others,
raids their cache of self-esteem, keeps it
deep in its rocky burrow just beneath
the loamy soil. It will never share or
mate with other narcissists.
It will eat its young.
But somewhere in its eyes you will see
a species that was once like others, surviving by
scouring the ground for love rooted and sprouting
beneath the brush, enough love fallen
from the trees
to sustain them all.

GOOD GIRL
BY SAMANTHA JACOBS

I will never miss the smell of winter now,
I'm haunted by summer low tide
Sweet warm rot of mango skins
Sweat on white sheets

In a place abandoned by progress
Staring up at you,
My thunder and sun,
My slice of earth,
Pretty mouth half open, eyes
Twin blue saucer-moons haloed in haze.
Move deep and honey-slow,
Teach me thirst to drain oceans.

When you go, I'll still taste you
In the corners of my mouth,
Hear the name you've given me
Caught in your voice,
A corridor echo
A hole in my sky.

BEGIN AGAIN
BY LAURA MADELINE WISEMAN

I.

Perpetual ache begins in the shoulder, that space behind the blade. Sometimes it travels to the skull or ties into a knot in the glute. The room is orange walls, soft lights, green mats. Peppermint scent drifts in the air. A voice guides bodies in the fitness room, if elsewhere others work. At class's end, she says, *You need a challenge.* Is this ordinary advice—massage, foam roller, sauna—or unusual knowledge—chakras, doshas, ayurvedic? She says, *Mine was hero.* Another, *Fire log.* Must there be a challenge? National bike challenge. Plank challenge. Century challenge. Holiday challenge. Fall fitness incentive challenge. Daily physically uncomfortable pose challenge. Then in the living room as the first snow drifts, step into it—twisted-triangle or *parivrtta trikonasana,* also called pain, failure to breathe, impossible to hold. Try one side. Does the pose look like a scarecrow, an aerobics star, a jitterbug? Try the other. Does perpetual ache count? Is a choked neck enough? Let go of what's physically uncomfortable just as the door opens with, *What are you doing?* Standing up, I say, *Just stretching.*

II.

Each day pose. Each day lift—curl, squat, fly, lunge—then do things with impossible names—diamond crunches, burpees, one-armed planks. Which class is today's—power pump, HIIT, spin? Workout, workaday, workweek, workaholic, workaround—what isn't work? In meditation, thoughts scamper like puppies but return to the breath. In the studio, another's mat claims a preferred spot but say, *Let me get my stuff out of your way*. In class, no one has done the research but everyone wants an extension. At the computer with the budget, the income covers utilities and food but allows shopping sprees only to the Goodwill—gym gear (10 for 10 dollar sale), work clothes (99 cent Black Friday sale), and home practice props (50% off red tag housewares sale). Then commute home, basket full of second-hand wares. Post-stretch, but the mind tangles—knee, hip, arm. Hover between fold and opening, wall and stair, twist and stretch. Who's twisting? What's uncoiling? Today when the floor is almost within reach, the door opens with a sigh, and I say, *This is not getting easier. Is that the point?*

III.

It's day 13 or maybe day 17. Why does it still feel like a beginning? Drag out props—chair, block, blanket. Study modifications—books, videos, links. Begin in variation. Modify. Then begin again. The mind is here. Then the mind ruminates. Then it's back again. This is the practice—not yoga, but mind control. Raise crown, tuck chin, lower shoulders to now. To be means to find again. Breathe. What's the point of this challenge? Not the discomfort of twists, chest rotations, arm stretches. Not what wiki says about correcting posture, relieving indigestion, toning spinal nerves. Not yoking home to practice. This is the challenge—not a pose, but a bearing study. It expands—body, room, encounters, city. *It's really snowing,* she says. *Do you want a ride? I can put your bike in my trunk.* Then bad habits reappear, old wounds, perpetual aches. But beginnings matter, the intention to notice, readjust. Rest a hand. Align the torso. Broaden the collarbones. Lift the heart. Switch sides. Bring hands to chest. Press thumbs into what breathes, that pulse. When the door opens with the swirls of yet another blizzard, I say, *It's good.* You say, *Oh, yeah?* I step from the pose, reach to you, saying, *Yeah today, the stretch felt almost good.*

IV.

Three weeks in, there's an opening on one day, then the next. Commute by bike, but add in training—cardiovascular, strength, intervals. Work, errands, gym, home. Build up to it—runners, revolved-side-angle, half-moon. Linger in hip openers—lizard, pigeon, butterfly. Then twisted-triangle, breath. Before, if the dad said, *Can't you see I'm busy, kid?,* he now shuffles with bad knees, slumped shoulders, swollen fists. When he answers, he says, *Not enough hours in the day.* Let him go. He's not the challenge. Prep dinner—beef, asparagus, blueberries, cinnamon tea. Over such riches, prep for class. In the morning, describe such a challenge. Teach—raise one heel, bend from hips, twist, broaden. Then flow. Share what comes of study—mythologies, translations, body types—but let them decide the meaning. Later at home when the door opens, you enter playing air drums, husky with the commute. I reach for your hand, then ask, *Would you like to do this with me? The week between Xmas and New Year's, the gym opens to the community for free.* You ask, *Is this a new challenge?* I say, *It could be.*

V.

The last days of the challenge arrive with thanks. Say it after the commutes, while loading the trailer with pre-holiday groceries, then driving to visit family. Say it because Mondays need motivation, Tuesdays need tips, Wednesdays need wisdom, Thursdays need thoughts, Fridays need Friends. Say it because there's Black Friday, Cyber Monday, Giving Tuesday, fiscal lines, shopping madness. Say it to avoid the mid-holiday dramas or post-holiday gripes. Breathe. Read that saying it changes the brain. Say it in email, on to-dos lists, over budget. When the bike gets stolen, and dad says, *You can have that old mountain bike in the shed,* say it. Then fix—chain, gears, bell—add—basket, chain-lock, lights. Say it when grades are turned in, late holiday cards arrive, entire evenings expand with whatever. Say it because the gym is free. Friends come. New students attend. Classes fill. Say it all the way to and through the final day of the challenge. Then the door opens. I wave you over to sit. I say, *The challenge is complete. If it did and didn't get easier.* Pointing to props, books, where the ache still comes, I add, *I learned to hear the story.* You ask, *Okay, so the challenge taught you to listen, but why'd you do it?* I could say anything, but say, *You're sweet to ask. I wanted to learn to breathe.*

INTERVALS
BY LAURINDA LIND

Islands our wider definition

    where we set water

behind us, want somewhere

    strange. When young we

struck offshore as we could,

    wandered the waves, we

were gulls. Cedars soaked

    the air out there, turtles

were our tribes, rockfaces

    and roots were maps

that rearranged us till we

    had to learn the dry life

again in boats that brought

    us, alien, back to the land.

CONTRIBUTORS

Alex Apuzzo is a twenty-one year old college student studying creative Writing at SUNY New Paltz. Previous publication by *Inscribe Media* and *The Chronogram*.

Jerrice J. Baptiste has authored eight books. She has performed her poetry at numerous venues including the Woodstock Library's *Writers in the Mountains* series in association with other noted female authors and poets in the Hudson Valley, NY. She has been published in *The Crucible; Typishly Literary Journal;* forthcoming *Autism Parenting Magazine*; *So Spoke The Earth: Anthology of Women Writers of Haitian Descent; African Voices*; *Chronogram; Shambhala Times; Hudson Valley Riverine Anthology;* Her poetry in Haitian Creole & collaborative songwriting is featured on the Grammy Award winning album: *Many Hands: Family Music for Haiti,* released by Spare the Rock Records LLC.

Lizzie Bradley is working toward an MA in Writing and Publishing at DePaul University in Chicago.

Originally from Pennsylvania, **Sylvia Cavanaugh** has an M.S. in Urban Planning from the University of Wisconsin. She teaches high school African and Asian cultural studies and advises break dancers and poets. She and her students are actively involved in the Sheboygan chapter of 100,000 Poets for Change. A Pushcart Prize nominee, her poems have appeared in numerous literary journals and anthologies. She is a contributing editor for *Verse-Virtual: An Online Community Journal of Poetry*. Her chapbook, *Staring Through My Eyes*, was published by Finishing Lines Press.

Wanda Morrow Clevenger is a Carlinville, IL, native living in Hettick, IL. Over 516 pieces of her work appear or are forthcoming in 160 print and electronic journals and anthologies. The first of a 5-volume chapbook series *young and unadorned – where the hogs ate the cabbage Volume 1* released in December 2017 (Writing Knights Press).

Diana Cole, a Pushcart Prize nominee, has had poems published in over 40 journals including *Poetry East, Spillway, the Tar River Review, The Cider Press Review, Christian Century* and *Main Street Rag*. Her chapbook *Songs By Heart* will be published in 2018 by Iris Press. She is a member of Ocean State Poets whose mission is to encourage the reading, writing and sharing of poetry and to create opportunities for others to find their own voices.In this capacity, she offers workshops in reading aloud and has participated in a number of projects to address social issues.

Jin Cordaro received her MFA from Fairleigh Dickinson. Her work has appeared in *Faultline, A Smartish Pace, Sugar House Review, Cider Press Review*, and *Main Street Rag*, among others. She is a Pushcart Prize nominee and recipient of the Editor's Prize from *Apple Valley Review*.

Maureen Daniels teaches English at the University of Nebraska, Lincoln, where she is also a doctoral fellow in creative writing. She is an editorial assistant for *Prairie Schooner* and *Western American Literature*. Her work has recently been published in *Sinister Wisdom, Neologism Poetry Journal, Gertrude Press, Third Wednesday* and the *South Florida Poetry Review*.

T.M. De Vos is the author of *Cimmeria* (Červena Barvá Press, 2016); a 2015 Sozopol Fiction Seminars fellow; and Co-Editor-in-Chief of *Gloom Cupboard*. Her work has appeared previously in *Tinge Magazine, Embark Literary Journal, MockingHeart Review, Vagabond, Folder Magazine, concīs, Juked, Pacific Review, burntdistrict, HOBART,* and *The Los Angeles Review*. De Vos is the recipient of fellowships from Murphy Writing Seminars, Summer Literary Seminars, and the Cullman Center at the New York Public Library. She recently completed her first novel.

Catherine Edmunds' published works include a poetry collection, four novels and a Holocaust memoir. She has been nominated three times for a Pushcart Prize, shortlisted in the Bridport four times, and has been published in many literary journals, including *The Frogmore Papers, Aesthetica, The Binnacle, Butchers' Dog, Crannóg* and *Ambit*.

Joanne Esser writes poetry and nonfiction in Minneapolis, Minnesota. She has also been a teacher of young children for over thirty years. She earned an MFA in Creative Writing from Hamline University and published a chapbook of poems, *I Have Always Wanted Lightning*, with Finishing Line Press in 2012. Her work appears in *Common Ground Review, Water~Stone Review, Temenos, Welter, Third Wednesday* and *The Sow's Ear Poetry Review*, among other journals.

Samara Golabuk is a Pushcart nominee whose work has appeared most recently or is forthcoming in *Bird's Thumb, Eunoia Review, The Christian Century, Inflectionist Review* and others. She has two children, works in marketing and design, and has returned to university to complete her BA in Poetry. More at www.samarawords.com.

Kate Hutchinson's latest collection is *Map Making: Poems of Land and Identity*. She teaches English full-time to high school students, but in her slivers of free time enjoys communing with trees and getting lost in poetry. poetkatehutchinson.wordpress.com

Samantha Jacobs is an alum of the MFA writing program at Manhattanville College. She has since traded New York winters for the perpetual summer of South Florida.

Oonah Joslin is poetry editor at *The Linnet's Wings*. She has won prizes for both poetry and micro-fiction. Her book *Three Pounds of Cells* (ISBN: 13: 978-153548649) is available online from Linnet's Wings Press, and you can see and hear Oonah read in this National Trust video: https://youtu.be/FXkca9vcUyQ. The first part of her novella A Genie in a Jam is serialised at Bewildering Stories. You can follow Oonah on Facebook or at Parallel Oonahverse https://oovj.wordpress.com/

A 2016 Pushcart nominee, **Mike Jurkovic**'s work has appeared in over 500 publications. Books and chapbooks include *smitten by harpies & shiny banjo catfish* (Lion Autumn Press, 2016), *Eve's Venom* (Post Traumatic Press, 2014), *Purgatory Road* (Pudding House Press, 2010), and *Blue Fan Whirring*, (Nirala Press, pending). Mike serves as President of Calling All Poets, New Paltz, NY. www.callingallpoets.net. Music features, interviews, and CD reviews appear in *All About Jazz* and the *Van Wyck Gazette*. His column, The Rock n Roll Curmudgeon, appeared in *Rhythm and News Magazine* 1996-2003. He loves Emily most of all. www.mikejurkovic.com

Steve Klepetar's work has received several nominations Best of the Net and the Pushcart Prize, including four in 2016. Recent collections include *My Son Writes a Report on the Warsaw Ghetto, The Li Bo Poems, Family Reunion,* and *A Landscape in Hell*.

Tricia Knoll is an Oregon poet whose work appears widely in journals and anthologies. Her collected poems include *Urban Wild* (Finishing Line Press), *Ocean's Laughter* (Aldrich Press), *Broadfork Farm* (The Poetry Box) and coming in early 2018 *How I Learned to Be White* from Antrim House. Website: triciaknoll.com

Sandra Kohler is the author of *Improbable Music*, (Word Press, 2011), *The Country of Women* (Calyx, 1995), and *The Ceremonies of Longing*, winner of the 2002 Associated Writing Programs Award Series in Poetry (University of Pittsburgh Press, 2003). Her poems have appeared in many journals, including *The New Republic, The Beloit Poetry Journal,* and *Prairie Schooner*. Born in New York, Kohler earned degrees from Mount Holyoke College (A.B., 1961) and Bryn Mawr College (A.M., 1966; Ph.D., 1971), taught literature and writing, and resided in Pennsylvania for many years. She moved to Boston in 2007.

Lenny Lianne is the author of four full-length books of poetry, published by two presses. Her poems have appeared in *Rattle, Poet Lore, Four Chambers* and other journals and anthologies. She holds a MFA in Creative Writing (Poetry) from George Mason University. Lenny lives in Arizona with her husband.

The winter dizzies New York's North Country, where **Laurinda Lind** lives and teaches. Some poetry acceptances/ publications have been in *Artemis, Ascent, Comstock Review, The Cortland Review, Main Street Rag, New Rivers Press*, and *Paterson Literary Review*.

Andy Macera is the recipient of awards from *Plainsongs, Mad Poets Review* and *Philadelphia Poets*. His work has also appeared in *Mudfish, Pearl, California Quarterly, Straight Forward, philly.com Poetry Quarterly* and other journals. A graduate of Washington College in Chestertown, Maryland, he now lives in West Chester, Pennsylvania.

Peter Arvan Manos writes a monthly column on renewable sources of electricity in *Transmission & Distribution World Magazine*. His poetry has been published in *The New York Times, Yellow Chair Review, Eunoia Review, Modern Poetry Quarterly Review, Atlanta Review,*

Provo Canyon Review, Avocet Poetry Journal, Parody Poetry Journal, Prolific Press, Elohi Gaduji Journal, and is upcoming in *Abstract Magazine.*

Diane G. Martin, Russian literature specialist and Willamette University graduate, has published writing in *New London Writers, Vine Leaves Literary Review, Poetry Circle, Open: Journal of Arts and Letters, Breath and Shadow, Willamette Review of the Liberal Arts, Portland Review of Art, Pentimento, Twisted Vine Leaves, The Examined Life, Wordgathering, Dodging the Rain,* has work upcoming in *Dark Ink, Wordsworthing,* and *Rhino,* and photos in *Conclave, Slipstream, Dodging the Rain,* and soon in *Dark Ink* and *Stonecoast Review.* She recently completed a memoir of collected, interactive nonfiction pieces.

Sarah Merrow lives in Baltimore. Her chapbook *Unpacking the China* won the QuillsEdge Press 2016 chapbook competition. Her poems have appeared in a number of journals, including *Naugatuck River Review, Passager, Broad River Review, The Courtship of Winds,* and *WORDPEACE,* and she has published essays in *The Flutist Quarterly,* a trade magazine. In addition to writing poetry, she restores and repairs concert flutes for professional flutists.

Lyndi Bell O'Laughlin lives in Wyoming. Her work has appeared, or is forthcoming, in *Nasty Women Poets: An Unapologetic Anthology of Subversive Verse* (Lost Horse Press, Fall, 2017), *Troubadour: An Anthology of Music-inspired Poetry* (Picaroon Poetry, 2017), *Blood, Water, Wind, and Stone: An Anthology of Wyoming Writers* (Sastrugi Press, 2016), *Gyroscope Review, The New Verse News, Picaroon Poetry, Unbroken Journal,* and elsewhere.

Carl "Papa" Palmer of Old Mill Road in Ridgeway, VA, now lives in University Place, WA. He has a Seattle Metro contest winning poem on the wall of a bus riding the streets in Emerald City. Carl, president of The Tacoma Writers Club, is a Pushcart Prize and Micro Award nominee. MOTTO: Long Weekends Forever.

Irena Pasvinter divides her time between software engineering, endless family duties and writing poetry and fiction. Her stories and poems have appeared in online and print magazines (*Every Day Fiction, Bartleby Snopes, Bewildering Stories, Fiction 365* and many others). Her poem "Psalm 3.14159..." has been nominated for the Pushcart Prize. She is currently working on her never ending first novel. Visit Irena at https://sites.google.com/site/ipscribblings.

Adam Prince's fiction has appeared in *The Missouri Review, The Southern Review,* and *Narrative Magazine,* among others. His collection *The Beautiful Wishes of Ugly Men* was published with Black Lawrence Press in 2012. More recently, he has moved into screenplays and poetry. His poetry has appeared in *The Pinch, Hobart* and *The Good Men Project.* He currently serves as the Stokes Visiting Writer at The University of South Alabama. More information is at adamprinceauthor.com.

Rush Rankin's poems are forthcoming in *The Yale Review, Confrontation, Hanging Loose, Mayday Magazine,* and *Hotel Amerika.* WorldCat shows that his meditation on aesthetics, *In*

Theory (Chelsea Editions, 2006), has been added to the collections of 111 national and international libraries. His other books include *Pascal's Other Wager* (Word Press, 2006), *Benedictions* (Vassar Miller Prize in 2003 for UNT Press), and *The Failure of Grief* (Nettle Media, 2001). His writing has appeared in the following magazines: *Antioch Review, Paris Review, Gargoyle, First Intensity, Triquarterly, Rattle, december, ACM, Pleiades, Seneca Review, Epoch, 5AM, River Styx, Shenandoah, Stand* (in England), among others.

henry 7. reneau, jr. (hreneau@ucdavis.edu) writes words in fire to wake the world ablaze: free verse that breaks a rule every day, illuminated by his affinity for disobedience, a phoenix-red & gold immolation that blazes from his heart, like a chambered bullet exploding through cause to implement effect. He is the author of the poetry collection, *freedomland blues* (Transcendent Zero Press, 2014) and the e-chapbook, *physiography of the fittest* (Kind of a Hurricane Press, 2014). Additionally, he has self-published a chapbook entitled *13hirteen Levels of Resistance*, and is currently working on a book of connected short stories. His work was nominated for the Pushcart Prize by *LAROLA*.

Joni Renee is an artist and writer from rural Oregon. Her art has been shared on such diverse stages as The Moth in Portland, the Segerstrom Center for the Performing Arts in Costa Mesa, California, the National Autism Center, and the MacLaren Youth Correctional Facility in Woodburn in partnership with the Morpheus Youth Project. Her writing explores themes of nature, family, and the body, and has appeared or is forthcoming in *Superstition Review, xoJane*, and regional journals. Her chapbook, *Your Full Real Name*, was published in 2017 (Future Prairie Press).

stephanie roberts has poetry featured or forthcoming, in numerous periodicals, in North America and Europe, including *Arcturus, Atlanta Review, OCCULUM, The Stockholm Review of Literature,* and *Burning House Press*. Born in Central America, she grew up in Brooklyn, and now explores reverence from a small French town just outside Montréal. A recent Pushcart Prize nominee, in 2017, she garnered finalist nods from a number of opportunities. Twitter shenanigans @ringtales.

Bruce Robinson walks the municipal golf course while all the golfers are at home. He swims alternately east and west in a nearby pool. He has encounters with working dogs, but that's outside the pool. Various intermittent rain delays have appeared in *Works & Days, Peacock, Right Hand Pointing, Yo-NewYork!, Pittsburgh Poetry Houses,* and *Panoply*.

Jen Sage-Robison is a feminist, proud mom of two LGBTQ kids and is active in the disability rights community. She believes everyone has important stories to tell regardless of education, background or literacy. She leads workshops with Amherst Writers and Artists and at Westport Writers Workshop in which she seeks to amplify voices not always heard.

Matthew W. Schmeer's work has appeared or is forthcoming in *Redactions, Poetry South, Slipstream, Sliver of Stone Magazine, Marathon Literary Review, Really System, Panoply,* *indicia, Slippery Elm, Surreal Poetics, Cream City Review, Natural Bridge, Valparaiso Poetry Review*, and elsewhere. He holds an MFA from the University of Missouri at St. Louis and is a Professor of English at Johnson County Community College in Overland Park, Kansas.

Ronald E. Shields lives in Rochester, NY. His work can be found in The Linnet's Wings and at poetryontherun.com.

Samuel Son is a writer with poems, essays and short stories published in *Cultural Weekly, American Journal of Poetry, Sojourner, Geeky Press, Mockingbird* and others. He is also a pastor in the Presbyterian Church of USA, working on issues of diversity and reconciliation. www.sonsamucl.com.

Paul Strohm was born in Montgomery, Alabama, to a career Air Force officer who took him around the world in 18 years. He married a Cuban refugee girl who can't wait to go home after the Castro brothers have died.

Ed Werstein, Milwaukee, a regional VP of the Wisconsin Fellowship of Poets (wfop.org), was 60 before his muse awoke and dragged herself out of bed. He advocates for peace and against corporate power. His poetry has appeared in *Verse Wisconsin, Blue Collar Review, Gyroscope Review*, and several others. His chapbook, *Who Are We Then?*, was published by Partisan Press. A full-length book is forthcoming from Kelsay Books.

Bill West lives in Shropshire, England, and is a Pushcart-nominated poet. He is currently an editor at *The Linnet's Wings*.

Laura Madeline Wiseman is the editor of two anthologies, *Bared and Women Write Resistance*, selected for the Nebraska 150 Sesquicentennial Book List. She is the recipient of the 2015 Honor Book Nebraska Book Award, a Wurlitzer Foundation Fellowship, and an Academy of American Poets Award. Her book *Drink* won the 2016 Independent Publisher Bronze Book Award for poetry. Her latest book is *Through a Certain Forest* (BlazeVOX [books] 2017). Her book *Velocipede* (Stephen F. Austin State University Press), is a 2016 Foreword INDIES Book of the Year Award Finalist for Sports.

ANNOUNCEMENTS

Our next reading period runs January 15-March 15, 2018. Submissions will be accepted into two categories: our regular submissions and our special themed category in honor of our third anniversary.

For our themed category, we have chosen the topic, "Threes". Many things come in threes besides *Gyroscope Review's* three years in publication: little kittens, blind mice, primary colors, square meals per day, sides of a triangle, wishes, lines in a haiku, strikes in baseball, number of dimensions humans can perceive, and more. Pythagorus considered the number three to be the noblest of all digits; it is the only number that equals the sum of all the numbers below it. So, with all this to inspire you, go forth and see what you can create as a poem for our themed category. Good luck.

As always, all submissions must come to us through Submittable (gyroscopereview.submittable.com/submit). Please read our guidelines carefully.

Stay up-to-date with us at our website, gyroscopereview.com, or find us on Facebook, Twitter, or Instagram. You may reach us by email at gyroscopereview@gmail.com.

Thank you for reading.

Made in the USA
Lexington, KY
17 March 2018